SEVEN
LESSONS
IN PURSUIT OF
EXCELLENCE

Order this book online at www.trafford.com
or email orders@trafford.com

Most Trafford titles are also available at major online book retailers.

www.TheJourneyofExcellence.com

Printed in the United States of America.

ISBN: 978-1-4269-7017-7 (sc)
ISBN: 978-1-4269-7018-4 (e)

Trafford rev.05/21/2011

 www.trafford.com

North America & International
toll-free: 1 888 232 4444 (USA & Canada)
phone: 250 383 6864 ♦ fax: 812 355 4082

DEDICATIONS

This book is dedicated to my Mother Nomsa Nomvete. Thank you for your prayers Mum.

CONTENTS

INTRODUCTION//

PASSION IS WHAT GUARANTEES EXCELLENCE

 You can only excel in something you love doing. It is not possible to excel on any work you do not enjoy.

> **EXCELLENCE** = (ASSIGNMENT + FOCUS) X PASSION
>
> **EXCELLENCE** = (SERVICE + FOCUS) X PASSION

Without Focus it is not possible to reach Excellence.

Passion is the quality that determines how far you will go to get excellent results. It is not possible to remain passionate about something you do not enjoy.

 Without passion for your work, it is very difficult to succeed, and to excel is unimaginable.

 It is easy to excel in an activity that is within your purpose in life. Therefore, the first step to become a Person of Excellence is knowing your purpose in life.

Excellence is the amount of action applied on an activity, or the amount of effort exerted on an activity to get better results.

Excellence is doing the thing right, and Wisdom is doing the right thing.

Any Service, any Assignment, any Task is an opportunity to demonstrate excellence, but to consistently deliver quality is only possible if you train your mind to be focused, passionate and maximize each opportunity.

Lack of focus leads to missed opportunities. When opportunities are seized, they become stepping stones to great achievements.

THE PROOF OF EXCELLENCE IS SATISFACTION

Excellence is applied on an **Assignment** or a **Service**.

Satisfaction is what you get when you have performed an excellent Job. Satisfaction is what your customer gets when you have given an excellent Service.

Your Personal **Assignment** in life, as well as any other **Service** has the following four Elements;
  i. **People:** Those who benefit from what you do, your Assignment or Service. Someone or a group of People, a Market or Customers to whom your Assignment or Service is aimed for.
  ii. **Problem:** Your Assignment or Service is a Solution to a specific Problem. It is an attempt to improve a situation or to meet a particular need.
  iii. **Opportunity:** Your Assignment or Service rewards you back with some Benefits, and the better the service the greater the Rewards.
  iv. **Place:** You can only deliver the best Service or perform well in your Assignment in a particular Setting, Environment or Geographic Place.

▢ **Excellence** is demonstrated through a **Service** that is motivated by **Passion**, given in a pleasant **Attitude** and performed with **Precision**.

▢ **Precision, Passion** and **Attitude** are the fruits of a mature character.

▢ Excellence is the Passion that is applied on a Service or Assignment to bring out quality results. Excellence is a product of Focus and Passion towards a Service or Assignment.

▢ Your **happiness** comes from what you **dominate** (your Assignment), and your misery comes from what dominates you.

❺ The Quality of your Service earns you **influence** over the people you serve.

▢ The Quality of Service you give today becomes the source of your **promotion** tomorrow.

▢ Excellence starts with an **Action**; Excellence is what you do with your talents, skills, abilities, dreams and goals. What God gave you is Potential, Excellence is what you accomplish with that Potential.

CHAPTER 01// FAKE IT ALL THE WAY TO EXCELLENCE

FAKE IT UNTIL YOU MAKE IT

The shortest way to success is to imitate success. The shortest way to excellence is to imitate excellence. Anything you can fake successfully, you can also excel at, and Excellence is enforced through repetition.

Peter Daniels an Australian and a successful professional speaker tells how he desired to be a public speaker but his dream was challenged by his severe Stage fright. He had to drink flour mixed with water before going on stage to stop his bowels from opening. One day he discovered that when he gives speeches to the mirror at home there was an improvement in his confidence. So he repeated the habit imagining in his mind that his audience was listening. It was not long before he was able to deliver the same speeches in front of thousands without fear and get a standing ovation for excellence. He insisted on acting like a professional until his spoof made him an expert.

You can model someone who is already an expert in your field by simply imitating them. Over time your natural actions adapt to those you are simulating. With time you will develop your own comfortable style and of course you will resemble your role model.

Modelling and imitating an expert reduces the time it would take you to become an expert.

 Act as if you are and you will become.

 Walk like you are in your desired role.

 Talk like you are in your desired role.

 Think and Act like you are the person you want to be.

With time your acting like will become a natural function to your mind.

When you start thinking and acting like a pro, you end up feeling like a pro. Even people around you start treating you like a pro. Think and act like you are successful, then success will be all around you.

Anything you do for the first time feels awkward and uncomfortable like the first time you rode a bicycle. You were uncomfortable trying to balance yourself on two thin wheels and still keep the bike straight at the same time. You must have fallen a few times, it always happens. Second and third time you wobbled a bit but before long you were riding that bike like a pro.

Sometimes you have to act like a fool in your effort to become a pro. After all there is a thin line between a genuine pro and a faker, so you might as well do it.

Your fear to look foolish is the only barrier that will keep you from growing.

EMBRACE YOUR MISTAKES WITH GRACE

Mistakes are an essential part of learning, they simply highlight where you need to improve. When you were younger you imitated your heroes for fun and had no fear or care what people thought of you, you left no room for embarrassment. Adults are too concerned not to make fools of themselves; But to fake anything successfully you need your creative childhood imagination, to let yourself go. The difference this time is that you impersonate yourself in your best performance, and stick with it until your fake act becomes permanent.

Just think, how many people you meet everyday who are complete pretenders; they act confidently yet feeling timid inside, some pretend to be personalities they are not, yet we accept them anyway. People may say things behind their back, but accept them anyway. People will say something about you too; in fact they are already saying things about your current state of affairs because people will always have something to say. So why wait, feel the fear and do it anyway. What matters is how you act not how you feel. No one really knows how you feel inside.

When Boris Johnson the fresh mayor of London started becoming famous, everyone thought he was a big joke; in fact the press marked him as an accident waiting to happen. He would pitch up looking scruffy on national TV for crucial press interviews which meant life and death to his dream career to become the mayor of London. At times his facts were twisted, often with an unrefined sense of professionalism, uncontrolled tongue and dry humour. At times he would make inappropriate interruptions during interviews but the only one thing by far clear about Boris; he used every chance he got to role play a potential Mayor of London with confidence. Whether he fitted the role or not was not his concern. Many times his efforts got messy ending up a big joke. But during re-elections for mayor of London, due to lack of best fit to replace the unwanted Ken Livingstone - the outgoing mayor, Boris became a suitable candidate. All the fooling around, acting the part and the trying hard paid off at once.

Your best training for your Position is during the faking. From the time you rise in the morning start greeting yourself and address yourself in context of your dream role;

"Good morning future Astronaut."

For the rest of the day stay in character regardless the comments of people and disapproving thoughts from your own mind.

REPETITION CREATES PERMANENCE

As the saying goes; Practice makes perfect. You become an expert in what you do daily.

 Efficiency is achieved through Repetition. The tenth time you do something is easier than the first time you tried it.

The *Three-Five-Seven* Principle states that the best performers in any field are people who have practised their skill for three hours each day, five days a week for Seven years.

Repetition makes an extraordinary activity become ordinary. Even if your skill does not become perfect with repeated practice, it can never remain the same, it will improve with each repeated performance. Any Art can be refined with diligent practice. **Repetition guarantees Mastery.**

The price of Mastery is self discipline, - a consistent effort to follow through a routine until there is significant improvement.

An R'nB artist once said;

> "I've got to practise everyday, if I miss a day, it's a shame but at least only I know about it, if I miss the second time my managers may find out and ask what's going on, but if I miss the third time the whole world will soon know about it and my bank account will show the evidence."

People who become experts are those who understand commitment and dedication. They persevere and stick to it day after day, making sacrifices until they reach a level of excellence that rewards them back for their sacrifices.

It is normal to flop up a new routine, but repeated trial and error with dedicated focus will make what seems impossible at the beginning become as easy as breathing. The first day a learner driver takes control of a vehicle, they endure the nightmare of having to drive through busy traffic. They sweat and fret trying to operate a vehicle and look at the road signs at the same time; it just feels impossible. Yet the same driver if you see them six months later they will be driving that vehicle listening to a car radio, eating a sandwich, chatting on a mobile phone, and still notice road signs and not bump a single car on the road. This is because all those driving routines that seemed impossible at the beginning no longer need attention; they are now controlled in the subconscious mind. This is true for any other routine, whether sport, art, learning a musical instrument or learning to speak in public. Repeated practice makes perfect.

DISCIPLINE CREATES CHAMPIONS

In one of my youth groups there was a passionate young lad, a High School rugby player - Mr G, as I nicknamed him. Mr G was driven. His dream was to be in the National Rugby team. He had to get up at five every morning, five days a week to exercise for two hours. He missed out on our Saturday youth parties because he spent his Saturdays either catching up on his school work or playing a game for his school against another school. Even the other youth knew that Mr G was above average focused and determined. While the other youth were partying, he was practising drop kicks and ball handling techniques. I asked him one day;

> "What gives you so much motivation to pay a price so big."

Mr G answered;

> "Because I love Rugby, I love the feedback I get
> from people when my school wins a game, and
> besides I really want to be in the National team
> one day."

I thought about it hard just how passion can motivate someone to pay such a price and make such determined sacrifices. If Mr G's desire to be in the National Rugby team was not so strong, there is no way he would pay that kind of price. I have no doubt he will accomplish his goal one day if he hasn't already.

 A strong reason will give you the strength to commit to any kind of discipline, if it is paving a way to your desired dream.

In the book of Proverbs the Bible says a diligent person will surely succeed. The diligent finally succeed. King Solomon, the most successful King of all times gave his seal of approval to diligence. So start faking your efforts towards success diligently until you reach a point of genuine achievement.

Usain Bolt, the Jamaican athlete who won three gold medals in the men's relay sprints in 2008 Beijing Olympics lives a lifestyle that shows his motivation is worth his wins. He counted his success in Beijing a blessing, in return donated 50,000 U.S. dollars to Chinese children who suffered from the earthquake. Bolt has become a reigning champion of the 100m race after cruising to what looked like an easy record breaking win in Beijing, and yet still broke his own record in 2009 Berlin World Championships. Did his success come as easy as it looked? Of course he puts a lot of effort to earn his gold medals. Bolt's whole lifestyle is organised such that it supports his performance. He maintains a strict daily diet, avoiding fatty food, sticking to proteins, vitamin C and liquids. As if that is not enough, he also maintains a routine of more than an hour of exercises doing frog jumps, bunny hops and hurls with heavy barbells. His track performance has earned him the nickname Lightning Bolt . Even though his discipline may look ruthless but Bolt confirms that any routine becomes easy like any other day activity if it is repeated enough times. **Performance gets refined through discipline.**

To keep to any discipline you need to have motivated commitment and a reason strong enough to justify the pain. If your reason is strong enough, nothing can stand in your way, it makes the price of discipline become insignificant.

What makes the finest experts is their exerted attempts, the extra rehearsal, the little extra effort, the ability to go slightly further when everyone else is satisfied.

CHAPTER 02// DEVELOP A MINDSET FOR EXCELLENCE

THE SECRET OF EXCELLENCE IS IN MASTERING FOCUS

Sir Isaac Newton was once asked to reveal his secret to having so many inventions, and he said;

"I think about nothing else but inventions."

He was consistently thinking of innovative ideas, so his mind delivered nothing else but inventions.

 What you consistently think about becomes your pursuit. You will become an expert in what dominates your thoughts.

You will reap your best harvest from an activity that you spend most of your time thinking about. According to the Bible where your heart is, that is where your treasures are. (Heart = Thoughts = Obsession)

You will reap your best profits from the activity you invest most your time doing.

What you focus on gets magnified, and will continue to grow as long as it is your main focus because focus magnifies.

You will become what you spent most of your time doing. "What you do daily determines what you become permanently" (Dr Mike Murdock, Author of *The Assignment, The Dream & Destiny*)

Since you cannot master everything, then decide what is priority to you and eliminate any extra unproductive activities. Decide what you will focus on.

Decide your area of Focus:

 Decide specifically what you want to achieve, that will make it easy to eliminate any other activities that are stealing time from the main thing.

 Decide which time wasters you will avoid, such as; not watching excess TV, avoiding unnecessary meetings and events that do not contribute to your goal.

 Manage your efforts to make sure they are concentrated together to contribute towards your goal.

Where there is no focus, energy gets diluted, and time gets wasted away.

If you are struggling to figure out what activities are essential to focus on, don't grow grey trying, simply read profiles of people who are successful in the area you are trying to develop. Read how they developed their talents, then repeat their steps. Adopt their habits and the way they do things, until you get an edge in your own performance, and you will certainly standout sooner or later. A good example is Olympians; Many Olympians follow a specific pattern of training when preparing for Olympics and their training routines are published on sports magazines and can also be accessed on the internet for free. To be highly inspired, find out also their sincere motivations and personal goals.

GOOD ATTITUDE BREEDS EXCELLENCE

Have you ever watched someone trying to serve from their area of weakness? Imagine someone trying to serve people when working with people is not their strength? They get so irritated by people, always stressed, unhappy and ready to kill someone. Their attitude sends out a *get out of my face* vibe. If they could, they would make you disappear. If you ever find yourself having to deal with such a person you are very unfortunate. The problem is that they are trying to serve in a wrong job, or they are working in the wrong place, or simply trying to function outside of their strength. It is difficult for anyone to function well in an activity that is outside their strength, and to excel is impossible.

 It is not possible to excel in something you don't enjoy doing. You can only excel in what you love doing.

If you work in a Customer Care job, in your Customer Care Training they must have told you to smile when dealing with a customer; Right? It is an expected point in Customer Care Training. It does not place conditions on when to smile; it does not specify you should smile more when you are having a good day, but if your boss has just been horrible to you it s ok to be grumpy. The instruction is simply-Smile! However, you can only do something well when you have an internal conviction of its value, its purpose and necessity.

Behavioural modification makes us do what is acceptable even if we do not believe in it. It is a shallow touch up attempting to fix much deeper issues. Only when there is an internal conviction about why one should act in a particular way will they show a genuine commitment.

Only when we understand the value and the morale for being nice to people then we do it from the heart not as a duty. Only when we understand the value of excellence do we show a commitment to excel.

 To have a good attitude is a choice and good pretence cannot replace a good attitude.

Once I attempted to book a hotel room online; unaware that my booking had failed, there I was pitching up at the hotel at the eleventh hour. When the hotel receptionist Zena realised my booking had failed, she knew I was facing a possibility of getting stranded in a town far from home. Zena took it upon herself to book me a room in another hotel entirely out of the kindness of her heart, using her phone and her time really going an extra mile. I was charmed and gave her a fat tip and said;

"Thank you, that was very sweet of you, it was my fault I didn't expect you to do that."

"You are welcome Sir, being polite is part of my job." She replied.

"No I don't think you are just being polite, that would be superficial, I think you are genuinely kind". I said.

People with a drive for excellence have a motivated attitude. It comes from strong internal values, beliefs and commitment to quality. Attitude is motivated by internal beliefs, and only a strong reason behind your actions can sustain your motivation. Without a strong reason, even good actions fall away when a testing moment comes.

It is one thing to be successful but another thing to remain successful. Success is sustained by keeping the right attitude.

The way you think and act is influenced by events and circumstances in your daily life, and therefore attitude is a response to how you interpret those events.

Your Attitude reflects in your comments, your behaviour, the way you think, the way you carry your body, your tone of voice, your facial expressions, all together the way you react to life. Attitude is a response; it is either a positive or negative response.

Excellence is a product of a Positive Attitude. It is easy to spot people with positive attitude, they have enthusiastic energy and are often cheerful, while people with negative attitude carry an unpleasant personality, always mourning and complaining. They see faults in everything, they speak doom, expect the worst, really not fun people to be around. Of course if you believe it is a terrible world, full of mean and nasty people, that is what you will get, - a mean world with monsters all over. Because of their attitude, losers expect failure, and see themselves failing and therefore become consistent failures. But winners expect success, visualise themselves winning and therefore enjoy the fruits of their Positive Attitude.

Your attitude sends out strong vibes; it either attracts people to you or pushes them away. If your dominant belief is that life is good, people are wonderful; you will have a smile and appreciation covering your face, warm words to say and sweetness in your tone of voice. It is your choice, whether you are going to carry a positive or a negative attitude.

Usually a negative attitude comes from hurtful childhood experiences. So we approach life in fear that someone else is going to hurt us, we build a mean shell to protect ourselves because we fear in case our childhood nightmares come back. People with positive attitudes may have had negative experiences also, but they made a decision to remain positive, regardless. They continue to see life as having a potential for good and therefore expect good.

 People of Excellence are not people gifted with a certain set of superior skills, but rather they are people with a set of Positive Attitudes.

Negative attitude can be changed, it is not something we are born with, it is something we have acquired.

ATTITUDE CAN EITHER OPEN OR CLOSE DOORS

As the popular saying goes - *your attitude determines your altitude*. Caleb's attitude towards the promises of God was an outstanding attitude. His story in the book of Deuteronomy Chapter One is a story of Attitude and Courage. He maintained a positive stand, believing that the Israelites who were short in stature were able to overpower the Canaanites who were massive in built. He believed positively in spite being opposed by ten of his colleagues. The ten other spies believed that they were like Grasshoppers compared to their enemies. Because of his positive attitude, Caleb and his comrade Joshua were the only two of the twelve spies who made it to the Promised Land, and the ten fearful negative minded spies died in the dessert. A negative attitude has disastrous results, but being optimistic can reverse the impossible.

Dr Norman Vincent Peale was a Speaker and Author with a message to help people overcome negativity. In his nineties he accepted an invitation to speak in a conference; though he could hardly stand on his own because of age, he gave an overwhelming message as he always did. Some brave soul came up to him afterwards and asked;

> "Doctor Peale why do you still accept speaking invitations at your age when you have already made so much money through your Books and Seminars?"

The aged legend smiled and replied;

> "If it was about money, I would have retired long ago, but there are still negative people out there, I believe I can change another life."

PASSION COVERS FOR LACK OF TALENT

Passion is a mental attitude that determines how far one will go to get results. Passion determines the level of commitment.

In any field, whether Sport, Business, Arts, or Ministry, passion is what distinguishes the People of Excellence. They work with precision; they perform outstandingly usually without even expecting praises.

☐ Passion always goes an extra mile.
☐ Passion takes care of details.
☐ Passion puts emphasis on precision.
☐ Passion puts an extra effort.

When talent falls short, passion never fails to deliver equally as good. In Ecclesiastes chapter 9 verse 10 the Bible says;
"Whatever you do, do it with all your heart."

Complaisance on the other hand will give any excuse to maintain Mediocrity;

"I am just not gifted, why try harder."
"So what if I'm a failure, I can't be bothered"
"I just don't care, leave me alone."

Such complacent attitudes only invite failure. They won't accept self responsibility, and people with such attitudes will at all cost avoid being accountable for their underachievement. Complaisance keeps people in mediocrity and is the number one cause of failure.

Limiting attitudes must be a terrible sin before God who has given us all the potential and abilities to excel. Some people go around life half committed in their attempts, handling God given opportunities with a weak grip and clumsy focus then wonder why they don't get breakthroughs and the promotion they are hoping for.

You can enhance your performance if you understand the value of Attitude;

PERFORMANCE = (SKILLS + EXPERIENCE) X **ATTITUDE**

P = (S + E) X A

To become an outstanding employee, a brilliant sportsman, being the best artist, the best mother, the top performer; your Attitude will determine your Altitude.

Performance Excellence is fuelled by Enthusiasm

Enthusiasm is a sense of excitement about the goal, a feeling of joy, an energy that is released from a sense of anticipation. Obviously one rejoices because they are anticipating something good, something worth celebrating, a new gift, an achievement, a new relationship, birth of a baby or some other outcome. But excitement can also come from acknowledging that life is a wonderful gift from God, a blessing, a privilege, an opportunity to be enjoyed. When we adopt such an attitude, that each day we are alive is a gift from God; that alone gives us enough reason to be enthusiastic.

Enthusiastic people are happy people; they show it in their warm tone of voice, a cheerful facial expression, the look in their eyes. They are relaxed yet beaming with energy.

CHAPTER 03// MAKE EXCELLENCE A DAILY HABIT

YOU ARE A CREATURE OF HABITS

"First we make our habits and then our habits make us." (John Dryden)

We are by nature people of habits. Our lives are guided by habits, we feel lost without them. We are always unconsciously drifting towards the habits we are addicted to. You spend your day busy doing your usual habits. In essence, your habits are the building blocks of how you spend your day, and therefore how you will spend your life.

 Your success or failure in life is determined by what you do daily. **What you do daily is creating what you become permanently.**

A combination of Good Habits can;
- Accelerate your Success
- Increase your Performance
- Enforce Excellence, and
- Accelerate your progress in all spheres of life.

You can reach higher levels of Excellence by getting addicted to Habits of Excellence.

 Bad habits can make your journey so slippery that you end up spending all your life recovering from your errors instead of advancing to bigger life. Bad habits can distract a Good Course, waste your Energy, dilute your Focus and keep you in a Holding Pattern.

The non-productive Seasons of your life can be traced down to your object of Focus during that period as well as your Daily Habits during that period.

BE IN A HABIT OF EXCEEDING EXPECTATIONS

People of Excellence make effective use of their time. They intentionally press on maximizing each day, treating each hour with value. Mediocre People don't see the need to maximize the day; they go through the day unfocused, unplanned and frivolous with no specific goal to achieve. Because they fail to make the most of each day, they also fail to make the most of their lives. Life is simply a collection of all the days one has. Each day is an opportunity to pursue with passion the things that matter to you. Each day is an opportunity to improve your skills, your speech, your talents, your wisdom and your relationships.

Martin Luther King Junior once said;
> "If a man is called to be a street sweeper, let him sweep the streets as Michelangelo painted, or Beethoven composed music, or Shakespeare wrote poetry. He should sweep streets so well that all the hosts of heaven and earth will pause to say, here lived a great street sweeper who did his job well."

High Achievers and People of Excellence have a drive to give their best effort each day and be the best they can be under their given situations;

☐ They radiate and maintain high energy.

☐ They protect their focus from trivial issues and set their minds on delivering quality on their tasks.

☐ They are charged with positive energy, self motivated and even become an inspiration to the people around them.

☐ They set high standards for themselves but they are not necessarily perfectionists.

Excellence has its own rewards;

☐ It brings profits in Business.

☐ It improves quality in a relationship.

☐ It brings promotion and recognition.

 The rewards for pursuing excellence are always proportional to the effort one puts to excel. And the greatest reward cannot be measured in monetary terms; It is what you become in the process of pursuing Excellence.

VALUE THE HABITS OF INTEGRITY

People respect someone who makes an effort to live up to their word.

☐ If you say you will come at a certain time, then come.

☐ If you say you will do something, then do it.

☐ If you say you will call, for integrity's sake pick up the phone and call. Be a pleasant surprise, not a disappointment.

If you are always giving excuses for failing to do what you promised, then you are suffering from severe lack of integrity and no one wants to deal with an unreliable person.

An excuse may sound reasonable to you when you give it, but to the person on the receiving side; it just shows you are not a serious person to deal with. If you fail to deliver as you promised, it makes sense to apologise, you may give a reason but never give an excuse, instead be determined to improve and do better next time. People may get upset at you for failing to deliver but will respect you for being honest. Integrity is very important when dealing with people. What makes great leaders admirable to us is their genuine sense of integrity.

If you are going to make a promise, first check if you are able to fulfil it, then do whatever it takes to keep your promise once you have made it. I learned as a Project Manager that if my Project will take seven days to finish, then I should only make a promise to deliver in ten days not seven. The three extra days allow me to either refine my product or troubleshoot any unexpected problems along the way. If all goes well, then I deliver in seven days making a pleasant surprise of three days early delivery.

The phrase having double standards is used to label people who are inconsistent. Today they come on time but tomorrow they are late. Usually such people also lack the integrity to call and apologise or explain their actions and therefore destroy their own reputation.

Choosing to be a person of integrity is choosing to stick to the truth. There is no greater freedom than not having to remember the lies you said in the past, and thank God we never have to remember the truth. The truth always keeps us free, free of stress and pretence. Integrity is being honest with all people especially with yourself. The problem with lies is that you need more lies to support the previous lie and lies just keep building up until you get completely entangled with lies, and you can be sure you will sooner or later be discovered.

MAXIMIZE EVERY OPPORTUNITY

To treat opportunities with care is a smart decision, and never treat opportunities with negligence. There is no limit to what can come out of an opportunity when it is managed well and maximized. When you give your best effort to an opportunity, it can bring you favour and even better opportunities, but treating opportunities with negligence leads to a downfall. According to the bible, if you are faithful with little things, you will be given charge over big things. If you respect the favour of those who bring you opportunities, they will remember you when bigger and better opportunities come along.

TREAT TIME WITH RESPECT

Time is the only resource that once used cannot be restored. It is due for a single consumption, it cannot be stored for later use; time is unable to wait. Each day comes once, with unique opportunities for that day.

Mediocre People say;
"It's just another day."

Actually meaning;
"I just don't see any difference between yesterday and today. And because I can't see the difference, I expect nothing new today."

Of course if someone expects nothing new today they will do nothing new today. But the people who take their Dreams, Goals and Assignment seriously understand the value of each day. They treat time with respect, they work with focus, chasing after their goals and maximise the day.

This is the major difference between Achievers and Mediocres; the ability to use time wisely.

If procrastination is the thief of time, then it does not only steal time but also opportunities, progress and money. The only thing God has given us full control of, is time. Life is made of minutes and hours. When you fail to use one day well, couple them up you have lost the whole year. A good steward of time accounts for how he or she spends their time.

 They keep a Daily Journal, recording key accomplishments of each day.

 They plan each day, charting out a daily 'To-do' list.

 They avoid idle moments and are always driven to make each day productive.

A working plan does not have to be perfect. Achievers are decisive people, they are ready to act even if the plan is not perfect. Excessive planners always procrastinate. Action cannot be delayed for a perfect plan or perfect time. The weakness of excessive planers and perfectionists is that they never act, they just keep refining their plan. **Excellence is not perfectionism.**

To illustrate the value of hours in a day; Just imagine your Bank giving you money to spend and they deposit it into your Bank Account daily. Your Bank cuts a deal with you that allows you to use as much money as you want in one day, with a condition that you will forfeit whatever you fail to use that day. And every morning the Bank will top your account up with a new allocation for the day. If this were the case, you would start planning well just how you are going to spend your money each day and maximize as much of your money as possible because you know whatever you don't spend will be lost.

'Play hard Life's short' was a slogan for a Cigarette advert back in the 1990s. I can't remember which Cigarettes it was but I remember the slogan. It got me thinking that Life is actually not long enough to accomplish everything; one has to be selective and prioritise on what they spend their time doing. Even in its longest term life is still short. Ask a 91 year old, they will tell you;

> "It feels like only yesterday I celebrated my 21st birthday."

Your awareness of the value of life determines your Priories. When we get to realize how short life is, we become motivated to readjust our priorities to only what matters the most;

- We change the way we think, improve on how we live, and even improve on eating habits.

- We start to think about maximizing each moment and each opportunity.

- We start to value our relationships more.

- We start playing harder and show better commitment to things that have a permanent value, all because we realise that what we have today is not going to be here forever. Your strong body and your strong mind will someday not be as strong, it's a fact.

- We begin to cherish our families because we realise that they will not be around forever, we start to see it as an opportunity to be able to love them while we have them with us.

POSITION YOURSELF FOR PROMOTION

In the 1990s there was a movie 'Short-Circuit' featuring a robot which escaped from a US Military Lab and moved into the community. While running away it met a girl who was sympathetic and took the robot to move in with her. While hiding at her house the robot picked on some of her Books and started reading especially the 'How to' books. The robot discovered that all human skills can actually be learnt; from cooking a meal, to driving a car and even romance is learnable. So it decided to make itself useful in the house and became indispensable to the girl. As a result she decided to keep it permanently because she could no longer live without it. Anyone can make themselves indispensable, and anyone can become a candidate for promotion by cultivating the critical skills required in their field of work or organisation where they work.

THE 9 LAWS OF PROMOTION

Test these laws, put them to work and see if they will not bring you promotion, practice them at work and apply them in your personal life.

☐ *Mind the details:*
Becoming faithful in little things is the first principle that brings promotion, then more responsibility will be given to you. Projects that hold valuable treasures are only assigned to stewards who have proved themselves by taking care of details. Excellence is the ability to pay attention to the details and focus on precision. Excellence is the ability to treat little assignments with great responsibility.

Excellence is giving 100 percent effort to the task at hand. No effort is too much and no detail is too small.

Everything you do deserves your full attention and effort. Therefore aim to deliver your best, and still strive to improve if the opportunity allows. This does not necessarily mean become competitive; it simply means strive to beat your own best record, or do it better each time. This will make you an expert and increase your demand within your field.

☐ *Present yourself in best impressions*
The first thing people see about you is how you look. People judge your potential just based on how you look. Clothes don't just cover the body; they communicate something. They make a statement about the person inside the clothes. It is true that God looks upon the heart, but unfortunately He is the only one that does that, people will judge you on how neat you are, how well coordinated you are, how decent or clumsy you look.

Clothes need not be expansive to be decent. What makes you attractive is not the brand label on your clothes, but how your attire suits your kind of body and how relevant your attire is for the occasion. Colours and style have a meaning too, don't be deceived to try and look so unique that you end up becoming a laughingstock. Wear clothed that blend with who you are and be comfortable in what you wear.

☐ *Invest loyalty in your relationships:*
Promotion is given to the loyal. Since your world already has leaders, the best kind of support they need from you is your loyalty. They need you to buy into their Vision and support their Cause. Your reliability will increase your chances for promotion and give you access to Authority.

☐ *Be Active:*
Be always visible, be active, **be available**, be flexible, and be productive. The next person due for promotion in any organisation is the one who is always Visible, Active and Available. It's the busy people that are given more tasks to do not the idlers. *Idleness* is the sister to *Irresponsible* and they are both thieves.

Open your eyes and lookout for tasks that have no one to do, and do them extra to your given duties. Notice the gaps and fill them. Every job, service or project has gaps but only visible when you look out for them.

☐ *Go the extra-mile:*
Enjoy serving, **go an extra mile**, deliver more than it is asked of you, do more than it is expected of you, and if you can afford, place no charge for the **extras** you give. Aim to be consistent in delivering quality service. If you do that, you are planting seeds for promotion.

☐ *Be a creative problem solver:*
Creative minds are admired and often given a chance to prove themselves. This is true in many working environments. Find a problem within your field of work and solve it.

Think ahead, be a contributor. Become a Problem Solver; when you spot a need or problem make yourself the solution. Promotion, Favour and Authority go to people who solve problems.

☐ **Be Result Oriented:**
Be productivity driven. Be able to work independently without supervision. Organise a plan to tackle your work. As much as you can, avoid getting into Holding Patterns.

Try and figure out ways to accelerate your work. Do it faster and better each time.

Being busy is not enough unless you show results for the time you spend on a task. If you sit down to work, don't allow yourself to be distracted. Get up ready to account for your busy-ness. **Don't be just busy, be Efficient and Productive.** Never confuse working hard with being busy. Smart hard working individuals don't just work hard instead they employ tools and strategies to help them become less busy. They think hard and work effectively. They avoid being held up in busy schedules. They hate time wasters, they are always trying to use their time responsibly.

☐ **Be ready to work hard:**
If you have ever been led to believe that success is just a matter of luck, you have been misled; hard work is necessary to attract luck. Lucky people have earned their luck. They work hard preparing themselves for a moment of opportunity. They position themselves for luck and therefore get lucky because **Luck is an incident where Opportunity meets Preparation.**

You are likely to be motivated to work hard if you genuinely love what you do. You can never work hard

on something you don't enjoy doing, as Confucius the Chinese writer said it;
"Find a job you love and you'll never work another day in your life."

Many people have a fear of hard work, which comes from a common belief that life is supposed to be easy. Because of this expectation, their mind refuses to accept hard work as beneficial. It immediately gives an alarm; "Hard work! No! Run!"

Unfortunately some dreams and goals do not come without hard work, they require a lot of effort. The Book of Proverbs Chapter 14 Verse 23 says;
"All hard work is beneficial, but mere talk leads only to poverty."

Also in the Book of Proverbs Chapter 6 there is an illustration based on the Life of Ants; Though Ants have no Leader, small enough to be squashed under a baby's foot, yet they organise themselves, work hard, gather their food in large supplies during summer and when winter comes, they are well supplied, fully prepared for a winter Season.

80 percent of any Success comes from 20 percent of best Effort. 80 percent of Output comes from 20 percent of Input. This is called 'The Pareto Principle' (also called the 80/20 Principle). According to this principle - 80 percent of Excellence comes from 20 percent of Effort, then motivation is responsible for the rest. Similarly; 80 percent of Effectiveness is due to 20 percent of relentless Hard Work.

☐ **_Take Time out to Rest_**:
The most unproductive time is when you are tired but pushing to do more. Not only are you not productive, you are also prone to making errors. It is also the time you are most vulnerable to stress, to catching viruses and fall into petty fights with your fellow colleagues. It is just never worth it. Sometimes the most productive decision you can make is to take time out and rest.

Book a holiday away with your family to a different atmosphere, refresh and clear your mind of fatigue. A holiday can surprisingly become the most creative time giving birth to new ideas and solutions to your frustrating problems.

CHAPTER 04// POSITION YOURSELF STRATEGICALLY FOR EXCELLENCE IN RELATIONSHIPS

IT'S NOT WHAT YOU KNOW BUT WHO YOU KNOW
THAT MATTERS

I had just started a small church ministry in a township of Duncan Village in South Africa, where I spent a few years. I honestly didn't know what I was doing; I only wanted to help the people and meet the needs of the community as I saw them. I didn't have any experience in church planting, I was just zealous. When Tim a prominent respected pastor of a big church in East London heard of what I was doing, he sent out a message for me inviting me to lunch with him. Not knowing what to expect, I accepted the invitation. On the day of our appointment, as I walked into his large well decorated office, the secretary welcomed me warmly to the lounge where I could see tuna sandwiches readily prepared. There were pictures of his achievements and awards covering the wall. So I was about to meet a man of greatness. I sat there waiting for him to finish his previous appointment. I had been given a cup of coffee by the secretary but it had cooled down while busy rehearsing my greeting. If you have ever been invited by a person of a high profile, then you know the temptation to impress runs immensely high. He finally came out of his office walking out his previous guest, winked to acknowledge he has noticed me waiting. On his coming back we greeted with a firm handshake, but he could tell I was slightly uncomfortable. So he chatted trivially about nonsense, giving me time to settle, and then asked me about my work at Duncan Village. He showed interest in everything I was doing, the people I work with, my personal life including my consulting business. Then he proposed to work with me closely as a mentor and friend, needless to say I was openly excited.

From that day on we worked closely together on many projects. My recognition in town went from zero to hundred within months. I got invited to speak in churches, many of which were by far bigger than by my group at Duncan Village. I would politely ask my hosts;

"So why did you invite me?"

Their answer was almost always the same;
"We see you work and travel with Pastor Tim, we were not sure about you but we know if you work with him, you must be good. Since we can't get him to come due to his busy schedule, we saw an opportunity to invite you to speak to our congregation."

One day I told Tim about this, he just laughed at me and said;
"It's not what you know but who you know that matters."

That was my *eureka* moment.

In essence, it is actually who knows you that really matters. In my case, because I was known by Tim, in the minds of people it meant I must be a reputable guy. In the minds of people it symbolised I was a fine credible man because Tim the man of calibre would not hang out with me if I was not. This was a lesson to me; that your connections need not say anything to recommend you, but the company you keep says a lot about who you are.

In general there's not much you can accomplish without involving other people. Yet if you join hands with people who are effective, those who are pursuing significant things, those associations alone will open many new doors for you. Even your reputation is enhanced by your associations.

Your connections have keys to your future, to your next move in life, and to your next opportunity. People you know provide **leads and gateways** to the opportunities you need. To be rightly connected is crucial, and to get along well with people will pave a way to your success.

Show the people in your life that you appreciate them, you care, put them first, be interested in them, they will appreciate you back if you genuinely care.

THE POWER OF ASSOCIATIONS

There are strategic benefits in joining a **right social clique**, to rub shoulders with people who speak 'your language', - the language of excellence. Like minded people are easy to find in social networks, business networks, social clubs and church settings. You cannot open every door by yourself, you will need other people, some people more than others.

Thomas Edison, Henry Ford, Harvey Firestone, Alexis Carrell, and Charles Lindbergh were closest of friends and successful business giants of the twentieth-century, and all became significant history makers. In the book *Uncommon Friends* James Newton recounts a lifetime of friendship with each of these men. He highlights some of the qualities that tied them together, which is their sense of purpose, desire to succeed and their love for new ideas. Everyone of them became prominent in some way and each became productive so much that even today they still affect our economic affairs even thought they are long gone. Whatever their interests were in life, their friendship is a proof that **friends drift towards a common destiny**. These men shared and created opportunities for each other. They went as far as moving to the same neighbourhood in appreciation of their friendship. Up until recently Ford cars would come of the assemble line only with Firestone tyres. Generally, opportunities are shared exclusively within a clique of friends. When one friend comes across an opportunity, the first person they want to share with is another friend. This is the power of association.

WHAT IS IT THAT ATTRACTS PEOPLE TO YOU?

Have you ever thought about what people like about you? For people to like you, you must have won their hearts. People don't just give friendship, they exchange it for something else they want from you. In the first 10 seconds of meeting you people decide if they like you or not, whether to keep as long term friend or to avoid you next time, as the saying goes; *first impressions last.*

Within seconds of meeting you, they make up their mind about you - whether you are honest or dodgy , shy or confident, fun to be with or miserable. What makes you valuable to people is what you mean to them, the enjoyment they get from being with you. Really, what they like about you is what you can give, not what you want. If they can do without you, then you are not necessary. The same applies to the people within your world, you are valuable for what you can give, not what you are looking for. And usually what people are crying out the most for is to be loved, to be accepted and appreciated.

People make a connection with someone they feel they can trust, people they feel comfortable with. We easily trust someone who presents themselves as friendly even if they are strangers. When people judge you as friendly, open and approachable, they will let their guts down and welcome you into their inner circle. Usually a friendly smile gives a hint that you are a warm caring person deserving to be given a chance and potentially a good friend. If you look at people in the eyes when talking to them, they associate that with being honest, having nothing to hide. People are attracted to genuine people, to sincere, transparent, peace loving individuals.

When people meet you the first time, they immediately look out for specific qualities to associate with you and create a permanent profile of you for future. So how you present yourself the first time you meet someone is a make or break encounter.

THE LIKEABILITY FACTOR

Being likeable has more benefits than being talented or intelligent. It doesn't matter how intelligent you are, if you can't get along with people you will be limited in what opportunities you can access. When people like you, they will do anything for you. They can give you access to resources, opportunities and promotion that you do not qualify for. The short cut to getting what you want is being in favour with those who hold it. When you have their favour, you may not even pay for it. In the Book of Proverbs chapter 3, the Bible associates favour as being a result of kindness and honesty towards other people.

Since we cannot effectively maximize our potential without the help of others, we therefore have an obligation to make ourselves likeable. Remember people don't have to like you, given a chance, they will find enough reasons to dislike you, without you even knowing about it.

One key to being likeable is **being generous**. Be generous with gifts and with words. Giving a gift to someone does not only have a potential to open new doors for you, it also opens their heart to your influence. Also a heartfelt word of encouragement or a genuine complement at the right moment will melt a hard heart and crumble defensive attitudes. By doing these things, you leave a pleasant memory of you.

If you want to get someone's attention, you must show an enthusiastic interest in them, call them by their name, people like the sound of their name. Ask them about themselves; ask them about their family, hobbies, work, ask them about things that matter to them. Simply feed their ego, show them you are interested in knowing about them. People are naturally selfish. They may not remember anything you said about yourself but they will remember what you said about them, that you showed interest in them. No one cares who you are, only that you care who they are.

Being selfish will only isolate you and deny you a chance to enjoy good friendships. If the last drink has to be yours others don't matter, if all attention must come to you, and if you dominate every conversation, in future people will find a way to avoid you. As the saying goes - *me me me is dull dull dull.*

The law of sawing and reaping says; whatever you give out will comeback in large sums. What you give out, you get back. If you help someone reach their goals, someone else will help you reach yours. What goes around comes around. If you give love, you will get love in return. If you give a smile you will get one back. If you are prone to helping others, you are doing yourself a favour, it will all come back when you need it the most. Besides, you would never enjoy your success if you were the only one successful unless you moved to an island.

What people notice about you even before they hear what you have to say is how you carry yourself, your self confidence, the strength of your voice, whether you keep eye contact or not, the firmness of your handshake, the general atmosphere around you and the countenance on your face. Though these issues originated from western cultures and differ significantly between western and eastern cultures but they are fast getting adopted as standards especially in formal environments and business settings. What you say counts less, your accent and how fluent you speak the language don't count as much. If you have some sense of humour, it adds a plus to your likeability because people are drawn by a good sense of humour. Though not everyone has a natural talent for humour, but you can learn to laugh, laugh at yourself and not take life or yourself too serious. That makes people feel comfortable being around you.

CHARISMA IS ATTRACTIVE

People with charisma are attractive people. Dr John Maxwell the Author of *Developing the Leader in you* defines charisma as - being other people minded. He says when a person with charisma walks into a room the first question they ask themselves is;

> "How can I make the people in this room feel good about themselves?"

While the person without charisma walks into a room already absorbed in themselves, thinking;

"I hope I look good. I wonder if they have noticed my new hairstyle. I hope they accept me."

People without charisma are inward focused, while people with charisma are outward focused. The person with charisma has other people as priority, they put other people first. They show complete interest in the affairs of other people. They ask questions about how others are doing and usually end up being liked because people like those who show interest in them. If you give attention to other people you win friends and earn your right to influence them, and even your people skills automatically improve as you continue to show love. Make an effort to listen twice as much as you speak and always watch your mouth; relationships are made and broken by words.

BETTER GOOD RELATIONSHIPS THAN HIGH INTELLECT

A Basketball team in the US NBA premiership once had a shocking encounter during their first team session of the season. Instead of physical training as they expected, that morning the coach decided to get the team chatting about life experiences and life in the premiership. The coach broke the conversation with an unexpected question asking the team what they believed was the most significant thing that has brought them the success they now enjoy. Everyone gave some technical reason such as - our playing skills, our ball passing technique, our team strategy. Unhappy with their answers the coach interfered;

> "Well, you all missed it. That was a trick question to find out what you value the most as the most successful basketball players in the country. The one thing that has contributed the most to your success is your folks. You cannot succeed without the support of your family and friends."

The players were left with their mouths open in disbelief, but the coach had made his point, - good relationships are more important than talent or skill.

Getting along with people will guarantee you good life, happiness and moreover a degree of success depends on how well you get along with others. Research on staff turnover indicates that people lose jobs more from lack of people skills than from lack of technical skills. Another research on IQ indicated that people who are good in dealing with people are generally more successful than those with high IQ. They get more done through their connections and delegate better than their intelligent counterparts. They are friendly, warm, charming and accepting of others, and are generally loved by people more than those with high IQ. People don't care how much you know, they only want to know how much you care. Ironically most people prefer to work with people they perceive as simple instead of intelligent. Much in contrary to the claims of the book *Beautiful People* which claims that beautiful people are intelligent people and are admired by everyone. On the overall, people skills are more essential than superior intellect.

CHAPTER 05// SEARCH FOR LESSONS OF EXCELLENCE IN EVERY RELATIONSHIP

GET A MENTOR

One of the uncommon moments of my teenage life is the day I met Gibson, a cheerful youth leader who had an ability to inspire young people no matter how wild they were. Gibson was ready to motivate everyone he worked with towards a purposeful future. The day I met him was an unwitting moment. I saw his music mini Bus flashing pass me with nice massive prints on the van's side panels. The side prints were so bright and enticing that I followed the vehicle to get a closer look. In my simple small town mind I was just keen to know if we now have a new band in town, and fortunately the van was stopping in the next block. Naively I greeted Gibson and told him I liked his mini Bus and would like to join his band, if possible. I didn't expect him to say yes, but he instantly invited me to come audition in their next rehearsal which was the following day. Little did I know that moment that Gibson would influence my future for the next five years. He ignited the hearts of every youth he came in contact with. Although Gibson was a busy family man, his secret strategy was to simply influence our thinking whenever he got to meet us, gently persuading us to think big until we got the message. I could never see myself singing in a band let alone in front of an audience, I just wanted to hang out with *cool* friends who drove a flashy van in town. But Gibson saw much more in me than I knew about myself. As the band performed from school to school I couldn't stop thinking;

"I must be dreaming! Me carrying a microphone on stage singing with so many ears listening! This is the kind of thing I do in the bathroom alone."

Mentors have the ability to bring out the best in you. They plant dream seeds. **Everyone is born with a potential, and a good mentor helps to give it an assignment.**

I often wonder when I read about hundreds of kids who are driven into crime, drugs, violence and others who are written off as drop outs in society, where are the Gibsons to inspire them? Mentors who would believe in them, believe in their potential and inspire them to be productive contributors in society. Mentors that can see in them what their own eyes cannot see, and help them connect with a purposeful destiny.

Everybody needs someone to believe in them. Mentors are people who are driven by the spirit of Leadership. They influence confidence into their prodigy. When someone you respect sees potential in you, it gives you enough motivation to push harder to prove that you can do it. The motivation that comes from someone believing in you will make you overcome any amount of self doubt.

The bible has many examples of mentorship relationships; Paul coached Timothy in his work as a pioneering young Preacher who travelled around starting churches. Prophet Ali mentored a young Prophet Samuel to the point that Samuel became a greater prophet than his Mentor. Moses mentored Joshua to lead the Israelites and complete the journey to the Promised Land that Moses had started.

Mentors are an inspiration, their dreams are contagious. A Mentor will deposit their skills, impart wisdom and experience into you and save you years of learning from your own mistakes.

To find a Coach or a Mentor is not difficult, only find someone who shares similar interests, someone who is going the same direction you want to go. Generally, like minded people attract. Ambitious people are attracted to other ambitious people. Experienced people are usually keen to share their experiences with someone who enthusiastically wants to follow their footsteps. A Coach or Mentor can bring out the best in you if you allow them to. It only takes listening, teachability and a bit of humility.

Most experts are more than willing to share their success secrets. Because by helping someone else succeed, it reassures them of how well they know their stuff. It gives them an opportunity to challenge the limits they failed to break by coaching someone else break them. The only limitation to learning from an expert is a limiting attitude such as;
> 'A know it all attitude' or
> 'I don't need nobody to tell me what to do' kind
> of attitude.

Such attitudes only cause the expert to prefer watching you fail rather than correct you. But a wise person loves correction; wisdom is the ability to see beyond the correction - a refined skill, a victory dashing winner that you will become. Any effective learning needs lots of listening and less arguing, hence we have two ears and just one mouth, so we can take in twice as much as we let out.

ADOPT A HERO

The shortest route to any Success and Excellence is to **copycat someone** who has gone the same route. There is an African proverb that says; The suitable person to ask about the journey is the one who has travelled it.
Why?
Because their experience qualifies them.

Most eastern cultures are still devoted in the tradition that elders teach the young, and the expert teaches the novice and it works perfectly well. If you can find someone who has done what you want to do, don't reinvent the wheel, just find out how they did it. Take them out for coffee and ask them what steps they took to be where they are. An old Chinese proverb says; He who asks questions will discover the whole truth. Your responsibility is to ask. You can either learn through your mistakes or learn through someone else's.

Smart people know the value of learning from other people's mistakes. They don't look down on other people's experiences and so they never trip on the same errors.

Learning by copycating a hero can pace you to the same level as the hero. Heroes are people we admire as experts in the field of our interest. With time, just through repeatedly pacing yourself with your hero, you too become just as good.

In our age of multimedia technology with videos of everything made available on the internet you don't need the physical presence of your hero. Multimedia has made it possible to learn from experts from anywhere in the world, and spend hours with them without ever meeting them. Buy videos and audios of your heroes in action, or search the internet at *www.youtube.com* for useful videos or find useful videos in other video portals for useful material you can learn from.

My younger brother Jephthah is responsible for my taste of music. When we were growing up I listened to all sorts of wild tastes but he was a refined listener. He would feel sorry for me listening to what he felt was a lot of noise and offered his music to rescue me. He was particularly passionate about jazz, which to me did not make any sense. His passionate talk about jazz often made me wonder if I was missing something seriously wonderful in jazz. He later went to a school of music, and become one of the legendary players of sax. It has been fascinating for me to watch him over the years; how he admired and imitated Kirk Whalum, an American jazz maestro. He used to buy every Kirk Whalum music available, listen to each song many times over and practice each song note by note. One day I asked him ignorantly;

"What exactly do you like about this Kirk Whalum guy that is not in other jazz artists."

He responded kindly;

"Well, it's a pity you cannot recognise differences in sax tones, Kirk has one of the best sax tones ever heard in the jazz scene. I am his big fan, he is my hero. I imitate his tone so that I can find my own, hopefully as good as Kirk's."

Few years later I called my brother for a chat, and he started bragging about his recent international tour and the artists he shared the stage with. Then he added;

"By the way Kirk Whalum was in town last weekend, we spent sometime together and even played together one of his songs. Kirk was really impressed with my playing. He said I'm a brilliant artist, one of the best artists he has ever played with. I told him; I owe it to you Kirk."

To have a hero that you can use as a mirror of your progress is vital to keep you inspired. It will place you at a higher level of excellence.

FLY WITH EAGLES

There is so much one can learn from good friends knowingly and unknowingly. To have friends is not just a matter of spending time with people who like your company, it goes deeper than that; Birds that flock together also fly to the same direction. People who spend time together end up becoming like minded, they are hooked on the same addictions and habits. It is the power of association. No wonder in the Bible days if someone was corrupt, he would be eliminated from the community together with all those who associated with him.

The company you keep plays a big role in influencing;
- Your lifestyle
- Your values,
- Your addictions
- Your dreams and
- The choices you make.

You become a replicate of the people you spend time with. If you surround yourself with people who are bursting with energy, busy pursuing big dreams, you are doing yourself a favour, because their energy will transfer over to you and you will be inspired to pursue your own dreams. If you hang out with ambitious people, they will influence your ambitions, you will share in their hope and be influenced by their drive. We are as brilliant as the company we keep; so to be the best you must hang out with the best. There is nothing wrong with asking the people in your life what they are passionate about, instead of talking about trivia and weather forecast.

To break through your limitations, surround yourself with achievers, dreamers, risk takers, people who are daring enough to break through their limits. Spending time with such people will advance your purpose.

Quality friends can;
- ☐ Influence your performance
- ☐ Stimulate your pursuit of excellence
- ☐ Sharpen your thinking
- ☐ Challenge your skills and
- ☐ Help you release more of your potential.

According to the Bible like minded friends sharpen each other like ion sharpens ion.

To be a star, you must hang out with stars. If you aspire to become an Eagle, then fly like an Eagle and definitely fly only with other Eagles.

LEARN FROM EXPERTS

One warm Saturday afternoon two brothers Lull and Hayden invited me to go fishing with them at Newhaven down the South Coast of England. We spent several hours tossing our hooks, waiting for a catch. It was easy to tell that Hayden was the fishing expert among us three, he was the only one going on about all sorts of fish behaviours. He was also the only one who made a catch late that afternoon as the tide began to rise. I was moving my rod prematurely all over the shore, just following the ripples. Hayden was relaxed and unwilling to try hard, his expertise was evident. I asked him how he managed to be so confident about where the fishes are. He replied;

"There are fishes all over, the only problem is that you have no experience in catching them. On a good day, I can catch in one hour at least two whooper Pollacks or Codfishes from these waters."

Of course Hayden was right; the one who has taken the time to develop his skill will in time produce plenty while the one with an average skill delivers nothing in his best effort.

A skill is very much like a baby, it grows, it needs to be nurtured, groomed, taken care off, and any skill can be developed until doing it becomes as easy as walking. To become a master, you have to be selective and focused, as the saying goes *The Jack of all trades is the master of nothing.*

Being selective is the first step towards Mastery. The more things you try, the longer it takes to master any of them. Experts consider specialisation to be the key thing in crafting mastery. Experts usually excel in just one thing, not many. You too can specialise, by first developing one of your natural talents, one of your *core skills* something that you do naturally with little or no effort. Anything that you find easiest to do is also easy to master. The masters in any industry command the highest incomes. You too can become an above average performer in your field if you are determined to polish your skill, then money, fame and favour will never be your problem again.

Read books written by the experts in your field and get a window into their brain. It will give you insight into how they got be where they are. You will understand how they think and how they do things. When you have their knowledge and experience, you will accelerate your progress and avoid making the same mistakes they made. When I am faced with big decisions or crisis in my work, I stop and think how would one of my heroes deal with this situation? Immediately I wear their viewpoint the crisis becomes a piece of cake.

LEARN THROUGH YOUR OWN ACTIONS

Obviously any skill you may want to learn should be relevant to your work. Serious achievers remain permanent students of their field. They know other top achievers in the same field. They learn from each other and even copy each other. They are familiar with the latest developments in their field.

 Familiarize yourself with the latest research in your field and be up to date with latest discoveries.

 Know the who s who of your field. Know who is doing what and how they are doing it.

 Pick up magazines relevant to your work and be up to date with the latest Jargon.

 Tune into a radio station that broadcasts within your field, watch relevant documentaries and TV programs.

 Acquire and accumulate relevant knowledge, making effort to use effectively every learning opportunity.

 Learn, learn, learn, don't kill yourself with hard work, skill yourself and work smarter. Remember, skill has the power to open new doors, bring you promotions, opportunities and favour.

Read information that is specific to your work. There is volumes of information available on all kinds of subjects, you cannot know everything even if you lived to be 900 years. Avoid wasteful information. No point reading about the sex-life of a mosquito when you are an engineer. That cannot increase your engineering skills. Remember you become what you read about.

One of the key reasons why you should embrace learning is the dynamic nature of your personality; Human beings are 100 percent dynamic, they are forever changing. You are continuously changing for better or for worse, and **learning is what keeps you relevant and in demand**. New knowledge will determine the direction of your change.

The world around you is changing just so fast, it demands a degree of **flexibility**. Everything changes with time, nothing remains the same. If you leave a fresh potato in your kitchen cabinet and go on holiday, after two weeks you will be welcomed by a distinct aroma notifying you that your potato has changed. You too are changing just as fast, and every industry is changing that fast as innovative research changes the way we work and the tools we use. This generation alone has witnessed so many technological changes that if you don't keep up with it, you become virtually unemployable. We cannot be rigid but change with the times, otherwise we become obsolete. If you don't upgrade your skills you become stagnant and quickly become useless in your field. During the credit crunch of 2008, the first people to lose their jobs were those with least amount of skills to offer.

Because of your nature that is forever changing, you are wise to take control of the direction of your change, not to passively watch changes occur. What determines whether you will be better or worse five years from now is if you take responsibility for your own learning. In the next five years you are likely going to be somewhere other than where you desire to go, unless you are driven by some goals and maintain a consistent learning program to keep you fit. Adopt the *Kaizen* philosophy, a philosophy started by Japanese to keep corporate employees in a learning culture. Japanese believe that developing new skills and self improvement must be continuous throughout life for the organisation to remain on the cutting edge of its industry. Learning must be a lifelong habit if you are serious about becoming excellent in your field.

CHAPTER 06// SET GOALS SPECIFICALLY FOR PERSONAL EXCELLENCE

WHY IT S NECESSARY TO ALWAYS HAVE A GOAL

 The only Reason People fail is not having a Goal to Pursue.

Most people grow up to be adults without ever knowing there is such a thing as goals, except of course goals from a football game. Parents who themselves are not pursuing any significant goals cannot possibly talk to their children about setting goals. More than fifty percent of what a Child becomes later in life is influenced by the lifestyle of parents; the rest of their values are influenced by the prominent values at school and dominant social standards in the community where they grow up. In a typical Public Education System, there is no such a curriculum that covers Goal Setting, so it is easy to finish school as well as graduate University without a single lesson on how to set and pursue goals. Yet goals are the key determinant whether one will succeed or fail in life and career.

Knowing how to set goals brings meaning to life overall, because the things we use to measure the quality of life such as;

- Happiness,
- The feeling of personal worth
- Achievements and
- Quality Relationships, are all experienced in a lifestyle that is driven by Goals.

For instance; If your Goal is to have a great marriage, then that gives you a reason and motivation to rise up early, make breakfast for your partner and children, go out and work for income so that there is money for an exciting family holiday and money to buy nice things that bring happiness to your marriage. It also makes you willing to work on issues that threaten the unity of your family; all because you are driven by a goal to have a great marriage. Without such a goal, you have no reason to do any of that hard work, and just as well your marriage is exposed to the risk of failure.

If your dream is to build a business empire, it gives you the motivation to work hard creating strategic relationships, making lucrative deals and generate as much profits as you can until your empire is strong and non-collapsible.

When goals are the driving force of your lifestyle, they drive out incompetence and the sense of emptiness. They bring meaning, motivation, happiness and even bring prosperity.

The first place to begin is knowing exactly what you want.
Then the next step is to determine how to go about getting it. For example, if being self employed is what you want, then;

- What kind of business?
- What services do you want to offer, is it consulting, entertainment? Be specific.
- What kind of customers do you want to serve?
- What returns are you expecting in return for your services?

Going back to the marriage example; If what you want is to have a wonderful marriage then:

- [ ] What would make a good marriage in your terms?
- [ ] Is it seeing your family happier, if so what would make them happier?
- [ ] What contribution will you bring to make them happier?
- [ ] What steps can you take to bring about that happiness?

There is no change without taking personal responsibility to bring it. There is no change until there is a goal. You cannot bring about change when you are shifting the responsibility for your failure to someone else. For you to get the things you want, you have to take the driving seat.

 The primary cause of lack, failure, incompetence and poverty is lack of personal responsibility.

Many people desire to have a better life but are not willing to take the steps to make it happen. They talk about it but don't want to take the responsibility, yet it is actions not words that count; actions speak louder than words.

Taking action towards your goal even if it s small steps is better than mere talk. All great Achievements start off as small action, hence the saying *never despise small beginnings* . The Chinese proverb says it better; *The journey of a thousand miles is accomplished one step at a time.* One step a day towards your goal is better than no action at all. **Take a step even if its small, great things usually emerge from small but consistent attempts.** Be diligent at it, a diligent person finally succeeds.

YOU ARE BY NATURE A GOAL-SEEKING CREATURE

You were created and designed to always be working on some goal. We become disorientated without goals. After God made Adam he gave him a goal - to give names to every creature in the Garden of Eden. Once you do not have a goal to pursue your progress becomes fuzzy and your life becomes a fertile ground for chaos. According to the book of Proverbs chapter 29, verse 18; The lack of a clear Goal to pursue leads to an unfruitful life, this is because a goal gives direction and without a goal to pursue, there is no direction. Without a goal to pursue there is nothing to focus on and that is a recipe for;

☐ Mediocrity
☐ Low moral lifestyle and
☐ Disorder.

In the book of Exodus, while Israelites were camping near Mount Sinai, Moses decided to go away and pray in the mountains for 40 days. The Israelites found themselves idling, so they started to mess around with idolatry, creating a god from gold rings and ornaments. They had lost their vision and motivation to worship the almighty God because their Leader who always gave direction was away. Where there is no goal there is no activity to keep busy with, and so irrelevance (*sin*) starts to grow.

When Samson had a goal he was motivated to fight battles as one man against big armies of Philistines and conquer them, but when he had no battles to fight he was so unfocused he could not even resist Delilah's deception. When David had retreated from his goals he started noticing another man's naked wife, even killing poor Uriah for his wife. But when he was focused on his goals he fought battles and conquered nations, when he did not have a goal to focus on, he could not even conquer his own lust.

According to research, goals will even reprogram your body clock. Your ageing gets delayed, your strength is renewed and your health gets restored if you have a goal to pursue. When you are working on a goal, you feel rejuvenated and excited. Many untimely deaths have been associated with people who lost their will to live because there was nothing to live for.

The focus of this book is Excellence, but if you fail to get anything on Excellence then get this one lesson, - Excellence is meaningless without Goals. The Pursuit of Excellence means nothing unless it is exercised in a lifestyle that is driven by goals.

The only thing that guarantees progress and competence is setting a goal and pursuing it. Pursuing a goal enforces a life of excellence. Whether you set a goal because you are motivated by fear or by rejection, whether you are motivated to get rich or to be famous, whatever your motivation - goals will give you a quantum leap in the journey of excellence.

 The greatest reward for pursuing a goal is not just its achievement, but what you become in the process of pursuing that goal.

Setting goals will stretch you to grow during the process of pursuing them. Even if you do not achieve everything you set yourself to accomplish but you will never remain the same.

To be sure that you don't waste your efforts; commit your goals to the Lord in prayer, He will guide you towards success. All success, happiness and promotion come from God. He knows what is good for you and is able to direct your steps when you allow him to.

THE PROCESS OF SETTING GOALS

John a 15 year old law offender was given a punishment at a Juvenile Institution to dig up a large piece of land and then break it down with a folk. John was shocked at the size of land, but the Juvenile guard wasn't going let him get away with it, he stood there waiting with arms folded to see him sweat it hard. The unforgiving guard was watching to see that the job gets done within the set time. As John stood stunned looking at the job ahead, it suddenly occurred to him that if he divided the garden into small squares first that way he can manage his task and would be easier to see his progress. So he sliced the land into squares and started digging a square at a time. Working square by square he dug through with determination. Even though he could not see as far as the end of the Garden, which was his Goal, but he focused on finishing just one square at a time without getting discouraged by the size of the garden, and so he completed his task at record time.

The common question people ask is about Goal Setting is - where do I start? People ask this question usually because up to now they have lived life being busy day after day without bothering about the bigger picture and the outcome of their day to day efforts. So they don't know where they are in their journey. They are not even aware they have already started hence they ask where do I start. The question to ask is - where are you now? And then where do you want to go? Where you want to go is relative to where you are now, just in case you are already there.

Pursuing a goal works like operating a *'Satellite Navigation System',* - A device commonly used by car drivers for directions. For this device to help you with directions; You must provide a *destination,* - where do you want to go? Then the device takes a few

seconds to compute the best possible route to your destination. For the device to map the route it must know two positions;
1. Where you want to go (destination) and
2. Where you are currently (the starting point).

It then selects the shortest possible route to get there, and then it starts guiding you vocally by giving you short instructions. It does not narrate the whole route at once. It gives simple instructions like;
"In 50 meters turn left"
"Take the next right turn."

The device speaks like this until the driver arrives at the destination. Much like this device, for your mind to reach your desired goal it needs to know two things;

1. What do you want to achieve? (i.e. destination) This could be; to have my own Business, to Study a doctorate degree, to write a book, to get ready for a marathon.
2. Where are you right now (the starting point) or what do you currently have useful to help you reach your goal (An Audit of your current resources). Your skills, finances, possessions, and so on.

WRITE YOUR GOALS DOWN

Human beings progress through life very much like a Ten Pin Ball. Even though the ball is round and the pitching slide appears level yet once you toss that ball, it just slants to either angle except straight to the target. You are going to be a different person in 5 years. You are more likely to get off target unless you have a written **chart of goals** to remind of where you intend to reach.

Since life has many surprises, able to take you to unexpected detours, it helps if you have your goals written down, then you can always be sure to find your way back on track even in the season of chaos. Chart your goals on paper to help your stay orientated with your own progress and use it as your compass. It is easy to forget where you were going unless you have a map that you can pull out and redirect yourself to the original destination. Having a little goals book can help you refocus and stay orientated. In this age of technology, you can have your goals visible on your mobile phone and even create a recorded audio of your goals and listen to them many times until you are familiar with your own goals, and be familiar with who you will soon become and the strategy to get there. This will help you have confidence in your goals and increase your passion in the pursuit. Be sure to listen to them many times over; Repetition improves confidence.

SET SMART GOALS

Good goals are SMART goals, goals that are;
    S-Specific,
    M-Manageable,
    A-Achievable,
    R-Realistic,
    T-Time framed.

Making your goals clear and **specific** is essential; otherwise any activity that occupies your time can be mistaken for a goal. If you want to lose weight;

- Then how much do you want to lose? Is it 5 Kg or 10?
- What is the ideal weight that would make you happy? (your destination)
- And how much do you weigh right now? (your starting point).

Knowing your Starting Point will help you know how far you have to go to reach your target.

Managing a goal includes breaking it down into small tasks that you can commit to do daily and weekly, such as; to drink two litters of water daily, to eat one bar of chocolate a week, to run 5 Km every weekend.

A good goal must be **achievable**. First set a small target, something that is easy to accomplish, and then increase your target gradually. Instead of trying to lose a whole 10 Kg in 10 months, see if you can work on loosing 1 kg in the next 4 weeks. In that way, you will not get discouraged. 1 Kg is more **realistic** in 4 weeks and easier to work on than 10 Kg in 10 months.

One mad day I challenged myself to cycle a trip of 120 Km from one town to another. After 80 Km I realized I was totally unfit to complete my journey, 120 Km had been an unrealistic target but I resolved to finish my journey anyway in spite my legs feeling numb. I changed my game plan; instead of trying to finish 120 Km, I only wanted to overcome just the next hill, and keep paddling without thinking about 120 km. Before I knew it I had cleared all the hills and reached my target.

Once the process of goal setting has been learned and mastered, and the lifestyle of pursuing goals has been internalised, it becomes easy to succeed in any venture thereafter. The process you used in losing weight will help you in saving for a holiday overseas. A businessman who has learnt goal setting while developing his business is better prepared to succeed in politics or any other attempt because the process is the same. After a mother has successfully mothered the first child, she is better prepared for second and third. Even though the second and third children maybe different from the first, but the principles learnt in the process of growing the first child are adapted throughout even to the grandchildren.

SET A STRATEGY TO ACHIEVE YOUR GOALS

A **strategy** is a planned process, a step by step guide to follow daily as you work on your goals from the start until you accomplish it.

I use a **POST** approach to tackle my goals;
  P- I define the **Purpose** for the Goal.
  O- I define the **Outcomes** and **Opportunities** to come from pursuing the Goal.
  S- I define the **Sacrifices** I would have to make for pursuing the Goal, or simply put - the cost of the goal.
  T- The **Time** it will take me to accomplish the Goal.

It is a habit of efficiency and effectiveness to plan first before you tackle the goal;

ACTION Break down all tasks into periods of realistic time such as weeks or months, with clear outcomes for each period and task.

ACTION Define the relevant stages and Milestones starting with the current stage - where things are right now.

ACTION Define how regular you will repeat each activity to get results; i.e. The Frequency and Schedule. Remember your strategy should be **flexible** and **adaptable** in case you meet unexpected obstacles and be forced to take an alternative route.

9 Resources to consider in preparing for your Goal:

☐ Finances required to achieve the goal.

☐ Skills, knowledge or courses relevant to the goal.

☐ Relationships with key friends, mentors and coaches.

☐ Vision document: A written mission statement and Game plan towards the goal.

☐ A list of reasons and motivations why you want to accomplish this goal.

☐ A list of people who will benefit from it.

☐ A Progress monitoring system, Key Performance Indicators (KPI) or milestones, a checklist of what has already been accomplished.

☐ Routine Schedule: A list of activities to do daily with start and finishing time.

☐ A List of Habits and Principles to adhere to.

CHAPTER 07//
USE FAILURE AS A STEPPING STONE TO EXCELLENCE

THE BARE NECESSITIES OF FAILURE

Many people don't reach their goals, they terminate their pursuit prematurely by giving up when they meet up with failure. This is because;

☐ They don't fully understand the 'Science of Failure'.

☐ They don't understand the Purpose of Failure.

☐ They don't understand that failure is a necessary part of the Success Journey.

☐ They don't understand how to respond to failure when it comes suddenly.

Failure is an inevitable part of success. Failure is just the flipside of Success like winter and summer, like day and night. One exists because of the other, you go through one to get to the other, **no failure - no success**. The two opposites co-exist to balance each other. The creator made one as well as the other. Same as all other opposites such as darkness and light, day and night, negative and positive, hot and cold, poverty and prosperity. The presence of one is the measure we use to value the other. The value we give to one is defined by comparing it against its opposite. Darkness means not enough light, but as soon as you introduce some light, darkness begins to disappear. We appreciate one side because of the possibility of the other. If failure did not exist, we would not be motivated towards success neither would we be able to enjoy success. We would not have something to measure it against. Without failure success would be meaningless.

Dealing with failure is part of the success journey. Those who never try have never failed but they have never succeeded in anything either. Not trying is a guarantee that you will never fail, however not trying is on its own a state of failure.

 The sooner you develop a mechanism to deal with failure and the right attitude towards failure, the easier your Success Journey will be.

Failure only means not enough success yet. We eliminate the one condition we don't want by introducing more of its opposite, until the one we don't want disappears completely. You get rid of failure by inviting in success. You gain one by rejecting the other because the two do not equally share the same space. You can eliminate failure completely if you continue to introduce as many success activities and habits until there are no traces of faiure.

 Failure cannot stop you from achieving great goals because failure is not final unless you let it be. In the final analysis, success lies in triumphing over failure. Just never let failure make the last move.

Once you start on the journey of success or excellence, you must continue to push through without retreating because its opposite force is ever ready take over. If your goal is to boil some water, you have to keep in mind that as soon as the heat is no longer applied on the water, the water will start to cool down again, then all your effort becomes a waste. The possibility that we can fail is what motivates us to continue working on success. The possibility that you can be trapped in poverty will push you to persist on creating prosperity, unless you are not serious about prosperity. The possibility of being caught up in mediocrity and inefficiency is what motivates us to consistently practice the habits of excellence.

Crises is a possibility in any environment, you know *Murphy's Law*; something somewhere will go wrong regardless if you are prepared for it or not, leaving you with no option to negotiate but only to respond. Problems come uninvited, usually when we least expect them. So the best rule is to **flow and be flexible**, if you lack the ability to flow and be flexible during crises you will suffer a neck-breaking knockdown. If you are rigid you will break or stumble during testing times, but if you are flexible you are able to bend and can survive any setback. Being flexible means conditioning your mind **not** to let temporary trials distract your focus from the big goal, instead keep trying until you succeed.

ALLOW REJECTION TO FIRE UP YOUR MOTIVATION

Failure has a sister called rejection, that hurtful feeling that comes when you are disapproved, especially by people you care about. If rejection is hatched long enough, it usually turns into bitterness. When that happens, you are really in deep trouble, because when bitterness settles in, it clogs your performance, reduces your productivity and even affects the way you relate to others. The funny thing is we get emotionally hurt not so much by what people say or do to us, but by our own interpretation of what was said or done.

You can choose to disagree with someone who is showing disapproval of you. If you allow yourself to feel rejected, you are choosing to side with the disapprover, therefore giving power to rejection to destroy you. But if you choose to reject their opinion of you, you remain unaffected by their opinions just like a duck in the rain; it never gets wet. It just shakes the rain off and walks away dry as if there is a layer of oil shielding its feathers.

Everyone will at some point be rejected and face the choice to hold on to the rejection or let it go. You may be special, but you are not exempted from rejection. Be ready for it; develop a rejection-proof mentality, choose to believe only what is good and true about yourself. Shake off any disapproving opinions about yourself, never allow your mind to review the junk that people say about you. Remember, in God's embrace you are always accepted, if that comforts you.

You can use rejection to your advantage. Many people who are today World Changers, High Achievers, Pioneers and Top Performers encountered rejections which motivated them to prove their haters wrong. To be on the cutting edge of achievement, they had to overcome feelings of rejection, they rejected the opinions of their haters and stayed focused on their goals. Some had to overcome memories of chaotic social upbringing and broken family backgrounds. They too were tagged and called such names as Nerd, Square, Goofy, OTTAG (Other-Than-Talented-And-Gifted) but they were determined to look beyond such criticism counting it as hogwash. **They refused to be controlled by rejection.** They enhanced their own self esteem, believing in themselves when no one would believe in them, hence they became tough minded winners far outperforming their critics.

RESPOND TO CRITICISM WITH A CORRECT ATTITUDE

The *Tall Poppy Syndrome* is an Australian phrase used to describe the tendency to pull down anyone who seems to do well. This is a common habit with Mediocres. Mediocre People find pleasure in watering down everyone else who seems to stand out doing something better than they. They get fun from watching people fail. In other parts of the world they call this behaviour a *PhD syndrome* - 'Pull Him or Her Down' syndrome. Mediocre people sit idling doing nothing but criticise and pull other people down, while the People of Excellence strive forward and get ahead. Somehow envy only destroys the envious while the envied continue to flourish.

Develop a thick skin against criticism. If you learn to understand the reasons why the critics act the way they do, it will help you respond better next time they open their mouth to criticise. But never take an offence from a critic or even spend your energy trying to figure out what they mean by what they say. If you are being criticised, check if there is any truth in the critic's comment. If there is, use it as **feedback,** rectify the issue and move on. To the winner criticism is only just feedback. Achievers ignore critics but welcome the feedback. If you use the pain of criticism to your advantage, it can help you improve, it can inspire you to greatness and transform your personality for better. Like they say; *feedback is breakfast to champions.*

Once you become successful, criticism is unavoidable, you become an easy target for critics because you stand out. Success attracts criticism. **Any lasting cause must also survive criticism.**

Instead of letting criticism break you down, dust it off and move on, don't review it, don't nurse it, don't rehearse it. If you do, you will end up bitter, thinking thoughts of revenge or worse of damage your self confidence. When criticism is allowed it creates self doubt and low self esteem. **Make it a rule of thumb to never remember criticism.**

CONQUERING THE FEAR OF FAILURE

Achievers are individuals who have learned to conquer the sting of Failure. They have developed the determination to get up and fight again and again without giving too much attention to the pain of failure.

Strong minds are created by failure, rejection and pain. An aeroplane needs a certain amount of wind resistance to be able to take off. Resistance is necessary to help us become strong. It is necessary to help us develop a winning attitude otherwise we would be in a constant state of slumber.

- Challenges invoke the resting energies inside to action.
- Challenges strengthen your character and purify your courage, giving you the ability to soar to higher levels.
- Challenges can make you tough just like clay is hardened through the fire. Tough minds are made in the heat of tough times.

Rocco a friend of mine once shared his formula to deal with offences. Even though his formula was related in the context of offences, I have used it effectively in dealing with rejection and failure, it works. Since Rocco realised that offences are unavoidable and bound to come one time or another, he decided to forgive not only those who have offended him in the past but in advance has also forgiven those who will bring offences in the future even before they do so. This creates an internal auto-response mechanism that when someone offends Rocco, they are already forgiven with or without an apology. I use this mechanism on adversity to stop myself from slowing down when I am hit by adversity. I take no time grieving over what could have been had things not gone wrong. Thinking this way is a waste of time. My auto-response mechanism works like a thick skin protecting my heart from getting depressed or regretting over issues that were bound to come anyway.

During a sport performance, a player gets injured but will feel no pain because his mind is focused on the action, but once he gives attention to the injury, suddenly it starts to hurt so badly that he can t ignore it after that. From that moment onwards the injury becomes the centre of focus not the game.

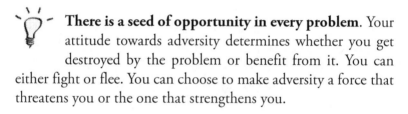 **There is a seed of opportunity in every problem.** Your attitude towards adversity determines whether you get destroyed by the problem or benefit from it. You can either fight or flee. You can choose to make adversity a force that threatens you or the one that strengthens you.

According to the law of polarity if there is a north then there is a south. Every situation has equal opposites. If the situation is very bad, there must be a very good opportunity on the other side of it. For every negative there is a positive. For every down there is an up. For every bad experience there is in it a potential for equal good. For every failure there is potential for same degree of success. So that means success is failure turned inside out. Your duty is to find out what lies on the opposite side of your tragedy, the advantage that is brought by the adverse experience.

Many great businesses were started by people who tragically lost their jobs. The worst experiences can turn out to have the best surprises. Stumbling blocks can be turned into stepping stones. Roses are hidden amongst the thorns just like opportunities come disguised as problems.

DOUBLE YOUR RATE OF FAILURE

Learning from your own mistakes is indispensable in pursuing Excellence. Life is a collection of mistakes, the more mistakes we make - the more we learn. So get ready to screw up and learn and increase your chances of success. The former president of IBM, Thomas Watson once told an aspiring writer;

> "To succeed simple means you must double your rate of failure."

In the same way; you will double your discoveries by doubling your mistakes. According to the law of averages; more mistakes means more attempts, and therefore increased chances of success.

Mistakes are part of our learning and growing. As a toddler you had the courage to attempt walking regardless how many times you fell, you refused to give up. You saw adults doing it and thought;

> "If they are doing it - then why can t I"

You tried and fell many times until you mastered walking.

From now on double your attempts to become a Person of Excellence and you will double your probability to succeed. When you make a mistake you discover the areas that need to be improved in your performance and you improve them.

Never fear to make mistakes, if you do, you are denying yourself the opportunity to learn and become a better person. **We make mistakes and then mistakes make us better people**.

FAILURE IS NOT FINAL

One morning I was feeling rather discouraged by a Business deal that would not go according to plan. Later that morning I called my mother for a chat. She sensed my down mood and tried to cheer me up, reminding me of my past battles and victories;

> "Do you ever stop to count your blessings, from where you've started to where you are now? You have come a long way." She said.

I paused, not getting what she was talking about and asked; "Why do you say that?"

> "Everything you have done up to now shows you are a fighter. You overcame all sorts of failures and rejections, you did not give up even when it seemed like all odds were against you; that shows you have a tenacious fighting spirit."

When she said that, I felt applauded, it was a nice pat on the back. It put the fire back on my belly, I stood up tall and said to myself;
"I can't allow this one situation to steal my joy.
I am a fighter not a loser.
I am more than a conqueror not a failure.
I am the head not the tail.
I am above and not beneath.
I am destined to win in any circumstance, over every trial."

As I repeated these words in my heart like a rhythm, I burst them out loud like a victory chant. I felt my energy getting restored. I regained my drive and spirit to fight forward. Not only did my mood change that morning, I started seeing in my mind's eye getting victory in my deal which had blocked virtually hopelessly.

 Success is certain only to the degree to which you are willing to fight failure back with Persistence and right Attitude.

PRACTICAL TIPS

GOALS

WRITE THINGS DOWN - PLAN ON PAPER. IDEAS NOT WRITTEN GET LOST. DON'T JUST THINK IT, WRITE IT DOWN.

KEEP A RECORD OF NEW IDEAS, DISCOVERIES AND REVELATIONS ON A DAILY JOURNAL.

TELL A FRIEND ABOUT YOUR NEW RESOLUTIONS AND NEW GOALS, THEY WILL HOLD YOU ACCOUNTABLE TO YOUR COMMITMENT.

DON'T WORK HARD, WORK SMART. MANAGE YOUR TIME BY MANAGING YOUR TASKS. USE STEPHEN COVEY'S TIME MANAGEMENT TOOL, (FROM THE SEVEN HABITS OF HIGHLY EFFECTIVE PEOPLE). GET MAXIMUM EFFICIENCY BY FOCUSING ON COMPLETING FIRST THE TASKS THAT ARE IN QUADRANT 2 - IMPORTANT BUT NOT URGENT.

☐ QUADRANT 1- TASKS THAT ARE IMPORTANT AND NOT URGENT
☐ QUADRANT 2- TASKS THAT ARE IMPORTANT BUT NOT URGENT
☐ QUADRANT 3- TASKS THAT ARE NOT IMPORTANT BUT URGENT
☐ QUADRANT 4- TASKS THAT ARE NOT IMPORTANT AND NOT URGENT

MAKE A DAILY TO-DO-LIST. DRAFT IT A NIGHT BEFORE. TICK OFF TASKS THAT YOU HAVE COMPLETED AND ALWAYS START WITH TASKS THAT ARE LEAST EXCITING TO DO.

EXCELLNCE

STAY PHYSICALLY FIT AND EMOTIONALLY CLEAR, KEEP A HAPPY SPIRIT, BE EXPECTANT AND STAY POSITIVE.

EVERYDAY IS A WONDERFUL DAY AND SO EXPECT WONDERFUL EXCITING THINGS TO HAPPEN. CONSIDER EACH DAY A GIFT AND DON'T WASTE IT. DECIDE TO BE AT YOUR BEST EACH DAY AND DECIDE TO ENJOY EACH DAY.

LEAVE EVERYONE YOU SPEAK TO FEELING UPLIFTED, INSPIRED AND HAPPIER. SEE GOOD IN OTHERS AND TREAT EVERYONE WITH RESPECT.

BE ENTHUSIASTIC, FEEL CONFIDENT, VIBRANT AND ENERGETIC. WALK BRISKLY WITH ENERGY AND STYLE.

SPEND TIME ONLY WITH PEOPLE WHO SPEAK POSITIVELY, AVOID CRITICS. AVOID PEOPLE WHO LOOK DOWN ON YOU, THOSE WHO DON'T RECOGNISE YOUR WORTH, SPENT YOUR TIME ONLY WITH PEOPLE WHO VALUE YOU.

GIVE EVERYTHING YOU DO YOUR UNDIVIDED ATTENTION. IF AT ALL POSSIBLE, WHATEVER YOU DO, DO IT RIGHT THE FIRST TIME.

www.The**Journey**ofExcellence.com

oscar.bonga@yahoo.co.uk

ACKNOWLEDGEMENTS

A special thanks to all my friends and supporters of the Journey of Excellence, I appreciate all your support.

ABOUT THE AUTHOR

Oscar Bonga Nomvete (MBA MSc) is a Leadership Advisor and Management Consultant. He facilitates Leadership Workshops and Seminars for Organizations, Churches and Corporate Companies. His Passion is to train people on the Principles that enhance Personal, Management and Leadership Effectiveness. He inspires People to become Leaders in their Careers and areas of calling.

He is the Managing Director of First Pinnacle LTD a London based Consulting Firm. He is an Entrepreneur and a Public Speaker.

BOOK SUMMARY

Excellence is highly valued by aspiring Achievers and thriving Organisations alike. People of Excellence are not born with qualities of Excellence; they become so as a result of pursuing the mindset of Excellence and practising the Habits of Excellence. Other than that anybody can develop the qualities of Excellence and flourish in Personal Life, Work, Sports and Relationships. 21st Century Organisations target individuals who exhibit these qualities, people who are self motivated, efficient and driven towards performance and productivity. People of Excellence are always looking for ways to do things better and faster and this book provides the tools and techniques, formulas and habits that one should focus on to develop the qualities of Excellence.

BOOKS BY THE AUTHOR

OSCAR BONGA NOMVETE

BECOME
an
UNCOMMON
PURPOSE DRIVEN
ACHIEVER

7 KEY STEPS TO BECOME
A PERSON OF EXCELLENCE

FAILURE
IS NOT FINAL
MISTAKES
ARE NOT FATAL

CHAMPIONS ARE BORN
FROM ADVERSITY

NO QUITTING

OSCAR B. NOMVETE

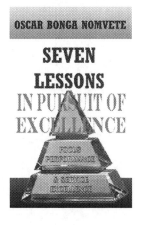

OSCAR BONGA NOMVETE

SEVEN
LESSONS
IN PURSUIT OF
EXCELLENCE

OSCAR BONGA NOMVETE

THE SECRETS
OF THRIVING
ENTREPRENEURS

A COOKIE CUTTER
STRATEGY
TO BECOME RICH

TOTAL FOCUS • QUALITY DECISIONS
LEVERAGING • THE SNOWBALL EFFECT

www.The**Journey**ofExcellence.com

PERSONAL NOTES

PERSONAL NOTES

PERSONAL NOTES